TOTES
RIDIC
TIONARY

Balthazar Cohen

Plexus, London

CONTENTS

INTRO DUCTION

"OMG!
That's Totes Ridic!"

THE INTERNET:
WHERE LANGUAGE GOES TO DIE

otes, *amazeballs*, *adorbs*, *obvs*. If you have an internet connection, chances are that you have at least a passing acquaintance with abbreviations such as these. And if you regularly spend time on social-networking sites like Twitter and Facebook, chances are that said abbreviations are either the bane of your life, or your second language.

If you like it, Beyoncé once sagely advised, put a ring on it. Online these days, it's more a case of: if you like it, put a hashtag on it, abbreviate it, retweet it, or Instagram the shit out of it. We're living through our phones and computers like never before, and, with little concern for sounding like speech-impaired halfwits, more and more of us are mixing up our typing and talking voices. (Particularly if we're aged between 16 and 35 and nurse an iPhone addiction alongside a mild drinking problem.) It's obvs totes ridic, but how did it get that way?

In the beginning, it was text messages. The average texter, whether jostling for space at a bar or on a train platform, running between meetings at the office, en route to the gym, or thumbing their phone under the desk during geography class, soon learned that brevity was the name of the game. Why waste your time executing six laborious button-pressings when two could just as easily suffice?

Thus, the population's time-starved and phone-addicted – or simply those for whom correct spelling had never meant a great deal – began using abbreviations and acronyms of everyday words and phrases in their mobile-to-mobile communications.

There wasn't a sentence or sentiment out there that couldn't be simpler, shorter, faster. Thousands of words and expressions were nipped and tucked to order. "Are you okay?" became "R U

OK?". "Great. See you later" was whittled down to "Gr8 C U l8r". "Have a good weekend" was sliced and diced until only "HV a GD WKND" remained. The dictionary went under technology's knife and experienced dramatic weight loss – getting the bikini body it had always craved, but at what cost?

Our global dependence on email only served to quicken the disintegration of the English language's self-image, and it wasn't long before the World Wide Web often resembled little more than a churning digital whirlpool of ROFLs, LOLs, OMFGs, FFSs, FTWs, and NSFWs* – one that threatened to rob punctuation-lovers and sticklers for spelling of their sanity. (*For the uninitiated: Roll On the Floor Laughing, Laugh Out Loud, Oh My Fucking God, For Fuck's Sake, For The Win, and Not Safe For Work.)

By the time social networking sites such as MySpace, Facebook and Twitter had successfully invaded our lives – used by everyone from pop stars to politicians – it sometimes seemed that abbreviations and acronyms were threatening to outnumber *actual* words, certainly online, but all too often in reality as well. Humanity spent half its time on the internet – gossiping, flirting, networking, self-promoting – but computers and phones alone couldn't contain the constantly-mutating dialect they'd helped create.

"Oh my god" (spoken) had become "OMG" (written), only, several years down the line, to become "oh em gee" (spoken). It became, if not strictly *acceptable*, then certainly not unusual to hear someone deliver a deadpan "lol" mid-conversation. *Totally* originally rose to bored-sounding prominence on the lips of Californian valley girls in the 1980s; now *totes*, its syllabically-slimmed down modern equivalent, peppers the speech of social-network users worldwide. The boundaries between internet slang and plain old slang have blurred. The minimalist half-language of the Facebook status update can just as easily emerge from a mouth as appear on a screen.

Thanks to Twitter's 140-character word limit, it soon seemed that – along with a thesaurus's worth of online acronyms – abbreviations (or *abbrevs*) were here to stay. *Obvs (obviously)*, *def (definitely)*, *jel (jealous)*, *hilar (hilarious)* – people often talked in the same way they texted and tweeted. It may have been ironic, or in the spirit of self-parody, or simply because everyone else was doing it – but whatevs, soon it was everywhere. In playgrounds and offices, in coffee shops and bars, on radio and television, you'd be hard pressed to find someone who hadn't heard or used the defining phrase: "That's totes ridic!"

So whether you're a 24/7 tweeter used to communicating solely through emoticons, or a self-confessed technophobe who thinks the English language died along with Dickens, you'll find something here to amuse you, inform you, or cause you to roll your eyes in recognition. Packed with an acid-tongued glossary of key abbreviations used by Totes Ridicheads, Facebook-addicted household pets, smartphone-savvy pop art, a totes-ridic reimagining of classic films, and the Twitter conversations of history and literature's most argumentative couples, *The Totes Ridictionary* takes a skeptical and humorous look at the absurdities of language in the internet age.

So put the "amaze" in "balls" and prepare yourself. It's time to become fluent in Totes Ridicularity.

TOTES
RIDIC
GLOSSARY
EVERYTHING'S ABBREVIATED

Abso: *absolutely*

Not to be confused with an ASBO (a British anti-social behaviour order commonly slapped on individuals prone to public displays of profanity and debauchery), *abso* is an abbreviation of *absolutely*. You might, for example, get *abso* smashed on Absolut Vodka. (Or whisky. Or tequila. Anything to numb the pain, really.)

"I abso love what you've done with this place."

Adorbs: *adorable*

Instagram photos of babies in cute outfits, Tumblr pages devoted entirely to pug puppies, Facebook albums documenting trips to petting zoos, Ryan Gosling generally – all these things are *adorbs*. Because, sometimes, the additional letters necessary to form its less on-trend older brother, *adorable*, are more trouble than they're worth. Particularly if you're about to go over your 160-character text-message limit.

"OMG! Zayn tweeted a photo of Harry sleeping on the plane! That's adorbs."

Amazeballs: *amazing*

An adjective popularized by celebrity gossip blogger Perez Hilton and beloved of people who aren't bothered if words don't make sense, or simply enjoy wrapping their lips around an unnecessary set of balls. When something is so amazing that it grows a metaphorical pair of testicles, it is *amazeballs*.

"Oh. Em. Gee. Kate Moss's jacket is amazeballs!"

Appaz: *apparently*

If you're spreading idle gossip that might not strictly be true – engaging, for example, in Chinese whispers about the sexual proclivities of that total arsehole from the HR department who keeps trying to get you fired; or unwisely repeating things said by Tits McGee, the constantly smashed girl from the bar whose real name no one can ever remember – you might seek to protect whatever's left of your integrity by qualifying the statement with a sly *appaz*.

Basically *apparently* with its legs chopped off and a *z* glued, *Human Centipede*-like, to its arse, *appaz* enables you to pass off information as probably accurate, while simultaneously allowing for the fact that you might be talking total bollocks. So it's no surprise that it comes in particularly handy on Twitter – spiritual home of errant rumour, wild accusation and falsely reported celebrity death.

"Appaz that is her original nose."

Atrosh: *atrocious*

Cheap-whisky hangovers. *Avatar* being the most successful motion picture of all time. Karaoke renditions of Katy Perry's "Firework". The spelling ability of anyone who has ever described a Michael Bay movie as "awesome". Such things are, as a rule, *totes atrosh*. Totally *atrocious*. Meaning extremely bad, completely crap, utter shit.

"I was stuck on a fourteen-hour flight with no films and nothing but a copy of Fifty Shades Darker. *It was totes atrosh."*

Awks: *awkward*

Undesirable social situations – like accidentally inviting your friend and her ex-boyfriend to the same party, even though they're totes not talking; or running into someone you know at the sexual health clinic – are *awks*. Gerald, the uber-geek from the accounts department who looks like his mother still dresses him, could also be described as such. (See also: *mawks* – as in *majorly awkward*.)

"Jennifer Aniston was sat near Brangelina at the Golden Globes. Totes awks."

Bestie: *best friend*

Nicole Richie and Paris Hilton. Gwyneth Paltrow and Madonna. Beyoncé and Gwyneth Paltrow. Harry Styles and Nick Grimshaw. Rita Ora and Cara Delevingne. High on fame and each other, riding a sexified tide of Twitter followers, brand endorsements and paparazzi camera flashes, these sleb power duos are all current or former *besties*, BFFs, friendz 4eva, best buds, bestest fwends.

The notion of having a "best friend" is arguably a rather adolescent and affected one born of playground one-upmanship, but sometimes the stars and people's shared career aspirations or drug habits simply align. Plus, it's handy to know in advance who you're going to call at 4:00am during one of those long, dark nights of the soul (generally involving ketamine and Jägerbombs) when you need someone to convince you that the prolonged existential crisis you call life is worth sticking with. #Bestie

"We do everything – and everyone – together. She's ma bestie."

Blates: *blatantly*

Originating in the UK, *blates* achieves its fullest potential when spoken in a thick Laaaaaaaaaahndun (that's "London", to the uninitiated) accent. It's essentially *blatantly* – as in *obviously*, *totally*, *yes*, *of course*, *I agree* – shitfaced on Stella Artois, brandishing a half-eaten kebab and looking for a fight.

Search for *blates* on Twitter, and your eyes will be assaulted by a churning cesspool of barely comprehensible bilge, one that squarely aims a shotgun at the head of Written English and, at point blank-range, sprays its brains all over the wall. This, alas, is the future. It goes without saying that no dystopian science fiction ever predicted anything quite as bleak. (Well, maybe *The Road*.)

"I've drunk thirteen pints and had three teeth punched out. I'm blates gonna call in sick tomorrow."

Brill: *brilliant*

Arrive at the bar just as happy hour starts? That's *brill*. Restaurant forgets to charge you for your main courses? That's *brill*. Your boss has two drinks with lunch and decides that everyone can take the rest of the day off? That's *brill*.

Brill is – like, totes obvs – short for *brilliant*. At least in theory. In practice, *brill* is splattered across Twitter's bowels with such frequency that it has ceased to mean a great deal. People are liable to describe damn-near anything as *brill*, even explicitly non-*brill* stuff – like finally managing to wipe away that annoying stray eyelash, or having a Starbucks barista spell their name correctly on their coffee cup.

So, unless you want to damn with faint praise, perhaps it's best to stick with *amazeballs* – it remains the one true means of simultaneously communicating enthusiasm and eradicating dignity. A bit like menthol cigarettes freshening your breath and shortening your life all in one.

"We had a long talk, and she said that she doesn't completely hate me – it was brill!"

Cazh: *casual*

People used to wear *casual* clothes, have *casual* extramarital affairs, and adopt *casual* attitudes towards personal hygiene. Now they wear *cazh* clothes, have *cazh* extramarital affairs, and adopt *cazh* attitudes towards pers hyge.

"Um, the dress code is smart-cazh.
Maybe rethink your outfit?"

Chillax: *chill out/relax*

Not a brand of toothpaste or oven cleaner, but rather the regrettable spawn of *relax* and *chill out*'s drunken graduation-night hook-up. Sufferers of stress, anxiety, paranoia or cocaine-induced heart palpitations will often be told to *chillax* by the kind of people who experience withdrawal symptoms if they have to endure half an hour without an internet connection.

"No, you calling her is what she wants.
Don't fall into that trap. Just put the phone down,
pick the bong up and chillax."

Convo: *conversation*

Convos used to be something you had face to face with another person. Then, in the late 19th century, the telephone was invented, thereby gifting humanity the power of instant long-distance communication, and the light relief of not having to look at whomever it was you were talking to.

But it wasn't until the internet and smartphones happened that the revolution really got underway. Text messages, emails, instant messenger, eForums, Facebook, Twitter, WhatsApp, BlackBerry Messenger, iMessage, Snapchat, Skype, Viber. Now the world can have utterly pointless and often downright disgusting *convos* 24/7, wherever you are, with as many people as your capacity for vigorous multi-tasking allows. (Unless, of course, you're stranded somewhere without wi-fi, 3G, or a phone signal – in which case, um, how do you live?) Our ancestors would be *so* psyched if they could see this.

"We had a long convo about how emosh unavailable he is."

Cray-Cray: *crazy*

Like the people it's so often used to describe, *crazy* spent a long time partying, getting messed up, wishing it was somebody else, hoping that one day it could maybe – just maybe – feel okay about being itself, feel comfortable in its own skin.

Tragically, that never happened, and nine months after one particularly wild, uninhibited night in Williamsburg, *crazy* gave birth to *cray-cray* – a sass-talkin' mini-me that technically isn't even an abbreviation, which soon infiltrated the tweets and Facebook status updates of high-school students the world over.

Things that might once have been referred to as "mental" or "messy" are often identified as *cray-cray*. For example: any time that an excess of alcohol and/or drugs is likely to be consumed. Or those disenfranchised members of society who view being humiliated on reality television as a viable career option. (Which, of course, it is.)

"Shit is gonna get cray-cray if that intern doesn't hurry up with my chai latte."

Dafuq: *what the fuck*

At the start of a typical Friday night, it's *what the fuck*. By your sixth drink, it's *what da fuck*. By 3:00am, at around the same time you start tweeting Beyoncé lyrics and searching for the nearest open McDonald's on your phone, it's *dafuq*.

Online, it's less commonly used than *WTF* – the prom queen of swiftly expressed surprise/disbelief/contempt. *Dafuq* often shows up in memes featuring pissed-off cats or Justin Bieber's face and in the tweets of teenagers destined to spend time in prison.

"She was all like, 'Four and a half minutes is not an adequate length of time.' And I was like, 'Dafuq? It totes is.'"

Deets: *details*

When more information is required – if, say, your roommate gets home at 7:00am reeking of booze and squandered human intimacy, or a colleague emerges from your boss's office weeping uncontrollably and promising to get revenge – you're liable to request *deets*. The abbrev is derived from the archaic, pre-iPhone word *details*.

"Mom, the One Direction tickets are about to go on sale. Can I have your credit card deets?"

Deffo: *definitely*

Like *definitely*, but with fewer morals, *deffo* is generally deployed in situations where ambiguous or uncertain answers simply won't do. It is often used to offer assurances to friends just before you change your plans and do something else at the last minute, because you're still quietly bitter about that time they left you waiting on your own in Nando's for *more than an hour* and, well, what goes around comes around, bitches.

"Yeah, I'm deffo still coming to Ben's birthday drinks."

Devo: *devastated*

Devo is the name of a new-wave band formed in the 1970s (whose song "Whip It" has defied the fate of most new-wave music by ageing like a fine wine), means *must* in Italian, and is now – most importantly for those seeking to effectively tweet wry witticisms at an audience of bored and indifferent office workers – an abbreviation of *devastated*.

Half the western world's tween female population would, for example, be *totes devo* if Harry Styles got married. David Bowie fans everywhere are left *devo* by the knowledge that he will almost definitely never perform his generation-defining masterpiece "Magic Dance" live. Lady Gaga is *totes devo* that, no matter how many meat purses or 32-inch heels she throws into the mix, she will never out-eccentric Tilda Swinton, druid high priestess of performance-art pretension.

"Lena Dunham didn't tweet me back. I'm beyond devo."

Diffs: *different*

Morrissey and his generation-defining quiff once pertinently enquired, "What difference does it make?" Had Twitter existed in 1984, the Mozfather might've sung, "What diffs does it make?" (FYI: the short answer is either "none", "some", or "lots", depending on how existentially adrift you are.)

Where once you found *different* or *difference*, you will now often find *diffs*. *Diffs* people, for example, are the unusuals, the individuals, the visionaries, the pioneers. Like Mark Zuckerberg. Or Susan Boyle. They roam free in the blossoming wilds of their own imaginations, rather than surrender to the dismal grind of running with the pack. Not for them a life of misspelled status updates about hangovers and the shittiness of the daily commute to the job that has left a withered husk where their soul used to be.

"I love that colour on you. It's so diffs from your yoozh look."

Dodge: *dodgy*

No, this isn't the word *dodge* – as in to dodge a bullet, dodge hearing the new Taylor Swift single, or dodge getting positive results back from your most recent Chlamydia test – but rather an abbrev of *dodgy*. As in: a bit unreliable, a bit suspicious, a bit risky – like a buying a "Gucci" bag from that bloke with no teeth who's always hanging around the bus stop, or choosing to give the twitchy girl in the club the benefit of the doubt even though the pills she's just sold you look suspiciously like paracetamol.

"My stomach is feeling totes dodge after that kebab."

Emerge: *emergency*

Not what a butterfly does when first wriggling free of its chrysalis, or the Fischerspooner song that invented electroclash way back in 2001, when the iPhone was still just a twinkle in Steve Jobs's eye – those are the old kind of *emerge*; the "actual" word you can look up in a "proper" dictionary. But knowing actual words from proper dictionaries isn't going to help you decipher all the abbrev-balled hashtaggery in your TweetDeck feeds, is it?

Emerge's Jekyll-and-Hyde alter-ego looks the same and sounds the same, but in a totes-ridic context is short for *emergency*. Granted, the kind of crisis the term refers to is more likely to require a friend to call your mobile halfway through a blind date and provide a wholly unbelievable excuse – burning house! Dead grandmother! – for you to get the hell out of there, rather than warrant the deployment of a fleet of ambulances.

If, for example, you overdo the carbs before a beach holiday, or accidentally enter the name of someone you're trying to Facebook-stalk as your latest status update, you are totes in the midst of an *emerge* and should deffo start drinking NOW.

"OMG! She's wearing the same dress as me. Retreat! Retreat! This is totes an emerge!"

Emosh: *emotional*

When Bambi's mother was shot. When Simba's father was killed in the wildebeest stampede. When Woody realized that a college-bound Andy no longer had any use for his childhood toys. When housewife outlaws Thelma and Louise slammed on the accelerator and drove off that cliff. When Sophie had to make her choice.

You may have described what you felt during such harrowing cinematic moments as "sad", "tearful" or "overwhelmed". In fact, what you were feeling was *totes emosh* – totally *emotional*. Like a father catching a first glimpse of his newborn child through breath-fogged glass in the maternity ward, or Gwyneth Paltrow balling her eyes out when she won her first and – let's face it – only Oscar.

When feeling *totes emosh,* you have a sudden, flickering insight into the beauty and fragility of human existence. Colours seem brighter; sounds clearer; the simple fact of each breath you take nothing short of a miracle. Then you decide that – fuck it – you will get the two-for-one deal on that expensive shampoo you like, *and* have a cull of all those annoying Facebook friends who keep posting pictures of their children online. Because you know what? You only live once. #Yolo

"He told me I was the least annoying of all the girls he's dated in the last six months. It was totes emosh."

Excluse: *exclusive*

Things that can be described as *excluse* (née *exclusive*) include:

- Places you want to get into but can't – like a *de rigueur* club gakked-up trendsetters are forever tumbling out of. Or that hot Starbucks barista's underpants.
- Monogamous relationships – like the one Gerard Butler has with making brain-searingly awful films.
- The photograph rights c-list celebrities negotiate with *OK!* magazine when they get married for the third time.

"The two of us are just having a good time together. We're not excluse or anything."

Fash: *fashion*

If the *fash* industry were a person, she would be an heiress with zero-percent body fat and fabulous shoes, her eyes radiating ravishing haute-couture deadness. Always on the guest-list at the best parties and visibly uninterested in anything you have to say unless your society or industry connections eclipse hers – which they of course never do – the Fashinator abhors animal-rights activists and any nutritionists insurrectionist enough to argue that half-chewed toilet paper and a packet-a-day Marlboro Lights habit do not a balanced diet make. But Anna Wintour bloody loves her, so, y'know.

"It's totes back in fash now."

Forevs: *forever*

"Forever," as Wendy Darling from *Peter Pan* sagely observed, "is an awfully long time." (So precocious, that Wendy: Edwardian England's very own Hannah Montana.) These days, a hip young pre-teen like Wends would've kicked that last *er* to the kerb and said *forevs*. Things of note that seem to last *forevs* include the films of Peter Jackson, flights to Australia, family Christmases, and k-holes.

"And then all the Hobbits started saying goodbye to each other AGAIN. I swear, that film went on forevs."

Fosho: *for sure*

Little in this world is certain. Buildings burn. Cities fall. Love dies. The thin gain weight. But if you're sure something's going to happen – like your train being delayed every goddamn Monday morning without fail, or your bank account resembling a particularly barren stretch of arctic wasteland by the end of each month – you can qualify it with it a *fosho*. Handy tip: if you write *fosho*, follow it up with an insouciant *y'all* for added urban realness.

"I'm livin' the 'merican dream fosho y'all."

Frealz: *for real*

When squashed into a tweet, like so much room-temperature salami sandwiched between white bread, *for real* often becomes *frealz*. Originally, the term was offered as a means of silencing disbelief ("No joke. I'm preggers. Frealz"). These days, people throw it into the mix for unnecessary emphasis ("I need breakfast in my body now FREALZ"), or simply because they can ("I just yawned SO loudly. Frealz"). See also: *frealzies*.

"This song changed my life. Frealz."

Frothin: *very attractive/very keen*

If used to describe a person, *frothin* means that whoever's doing the describing thinks that person is a hot piece with whom they wouldn't mind exchanging some intimate bodily fluids, should such an opportunity present itself. If used to describe a feeling – "I'm frothin about the party tonight" – it denotes excitement and anticipation, the pre-emptive tingle of knowing that shit is about to go down. A bit like how you feel after dropping ecstasy, but before it kicks in. Or when someone you know is easy agrees to go on a date with you.

"I would so hit that. She's totes frothin."

Gorge: *gorgeous*

Nope, not that thing compulsive binge-eaters do – generally involving a locked bathroom door, a KFC family bucket and as much of Pizza Hut's all-you-can-eat buffet as they were able to carry – that's gorging. In totes-ridic parlance, to be *gorge* is to exist on an exalted aesthetic plane of physical perfection, and most probably land a recurring lead role in the unrelentingly grim sexual fantasies of people far less attractive than you.

But calling someone *gorge* isn't just another way of saying that you'd damn well take a bite out of *that* apple, given half a chance. It can also denote great taste ("Those shoes are gorge!"), totes-mega-super-cuteness ("Oh em gee! That baby is too gorge!"), or something otherwise worthy of positive-but-vague assessment ("Babes, your wedding speech was *so* gorge!"). Some people throw shit and see what sticks. Others throw *gorge*.

"O to the M to the G, Nicole looks gorge on X Factor tonight!"

Hilar: *hilarious*

Hilarious, derived from the Latin *hilarus*, has been well known to English speakers since around 1840, but totally lost its shit after dropping acid at Burning Man back in 2007. When it finally managed to extricate itself from the overflowing portable toilet that had become its temporary home and piece together the fragments of its shattered psyche, it was *hilar*. Deployed nearly every time a teenager becomes mildly excited, its popularity in the Twitterverse is such that it is often used inaccurately – e.g. to describe the comedies of Jennifer Aniston.

*"LOLOCAUST. The 'Gangnam Style'
video is totes hilar!"*

Hundo: *hundred*

Rarely used by anyone who's already emerged from the slimy cocoon of adolescence, *hundo* is how twouths (Twitter youths) simultaneously say *hundred* and communicate their total disregard for the whys and wherefores of real language. It enjoys moderate popularity in hashtag form, e.g. "What are the chances I'm gonna get so drunk I can't remember a thing tonight? #hundo%".

"Can you lend me a hundo dollars?"

Imports: *important*

Nothing to do with goods and produce – including pillars of civilization like iPhones, condoms and red wine – being imported from one country to another, *imports* is tweetable shorthand for *important*. *Imports* decisions you encounter on a daily basis include choosing what kind of Instagram filters to use on photos of your lunch (e.g. will this pizza look more tantalizing in Lo-Fi or Nashville?), and whether or not to mark yourself down as "attending" on the Facebook party event of that weird drunk guy you met once and feel a bit sorry for, even though you know your presence is about as likely as Gwyneth Paltrow being humble while eating McDonald's.

"He's not answering his phone and we're completely out of gluten-free waffles! This is totes imports!"

Impresh: *impression*

As the saying goes, you only get one chance to make a first *impresh* – whether you're at a job interview, on a first date, or encountering new neighbours. Common advice given regarding the making of a first *impression* is to "just be yourself". It goes without saying that this is an utter crock of shit, and you should go out of your way to be anything or anyone *but* yourself unless you want to end up alone, unemployed, or doing jail time.

*"I kinda got the impresh that she wasn't that into me…
She said she was going to the toilet
and didn't come back."*

Inappropes: *inappropriate*

Whenever Charlie Sheen speaks; whenever Terry Richardson takes a photo; whenever Amanda Bynes sends a tweet, there is a 95 percent chance that the results will be *totes inappropes – totally inappropriate*. Like President Clinton's "relations" with Monica Lewinsky. Or any film made with the involvement of Harmony Korine.

As well as being a great way of finding out which celebrities can't punctuate worth a damn, Twitter is also a festering hive mind of *inappropes* sentiments. If someone in the public eye dies, gets arrested, or – better yet – gets caught in flagrante delicto with a sex worker, said website will gorge on the news like a starving man sinking his teeth into the flesh of a freshly roasted suckling pig. There follows a churning miasma of puns, quips, and droll one-liners. *Inappropes*, perhaps, but great for da lolz.

"I mean, he used to be her teacher – it's totes inappropes."

Inevs: *inevitable, inevitably*

Sunrise, gravity, ageing, death, hangovers, plane food being disgusting, the existence of internet trolls – these are just a few of life's inevitabilities. Other things that can accurately be deemed *inevs*: the rise of property prices, politicians breaking 98 percent of the promises they make to the voting public, and having "one more drink" at eleven o'clock on a Wednesday night always seeming like a *great* idea at the time.

"It was inevs that he'd get fired at some point."

Jel: *jealous, jealousy*

That green-eyed monster, *jealousy*, is back. And it's half the man it used to be. To tell someone you are *jel* is often a way of paying them a grudging compliment, or else casually referencing your own crippling sense of inadequacy.

"You're engaged? Wow. Congrats, hun. I'm well jel."

Ledge: *legend*

No, not something you stand on while contemplating suicide. To show respect, offer praise or express admiration, choose *ledge* – the drunker, ballsier, manlier alternative to *legend*. British uber-geezer Danny Dyer has it written through him like Brighton through a stick of rock. If you cut him, he'd bleed *ledge*.

"Wahey! Did you see that goal?
What an utter ledge."

Legit: *legitimate*

Legit – as in authentic, lawful, logical. For example, a *legit* criticism of the internet is that, as well as gifting its users entertainment, up-to-the-minute news, regular displays of rapier wit, and genuinely arousing homemade pornography, it also provides millions of assholes with a means of venting unoriginal spleen from behind the relative safety of a computer screen.

Anyone who wants their dismal view of humanity reaffirming need only glance at the reader comments threads typically found beneath online articles. "Kristen Stewart's acting is just like her appearance: very bland and instantly forgettable." Thank you, Keith from Ontario. Your pearls of wisdom are always hungrily received.

"I'm the legit heir to the throne.
And my reign is gonna be totes amazeballs."

Magnif: *magnificent*

Magnif is short for *magnificent*, a word one imagines Baz Luhrmann uses frequently when directing his lurid cinematic eyegasms. "No, Leo. Move over there, so the bejewelled strippers and glitter cannon are in shot. Now look into the camera and *yearn*. Magnificently!"

Consequently, *magnif* is a higher class of tweev (Twitter abbrev), often used by those seeking to succinctly convey the epic grandeur of, say, a football match ("Whatta result! The boys were magnif"), or hip-thrustin' arena-pop spectacle ("OMG! Beyoncé was magnif tonite!").

"Then she threw a drink in his face and called the whole thing off. It was magnif!"

Marv: *marvellous*

Men named Marvin are often called "Marv" by their friends from the barber shop. But this isn't about Marv, that grizzled old stoat, it's about being *marvellous* without the burden of those extra letters. Like a glass of chilled champagne at sunset, a Mozart concerto streamed on an iPad, a bathroom-mirror selfie you took getting more than 100 likes on Facebook, or checking your phone and discovering that you *didn't* send those SHOUTY, SWEARY drunk texts to your colleague after all. Marv, just marv.

"The hair, the dress, the dumb-but-gorge 25-year-old on your arm. It's all so marv, darling."

Maybs: *maybe*

A *maybs* hangs, Sword of Damocles-like, over most of life's indecisions and uncertainties. *Maybs* you'll apply for that job, or go to that party, or get that weird lump checked out by a doctor. *Maybs* you won't ever find true love, or own property, or earn a living doing something you don't despise. That's for the gods – or at the very least a cold, indifferent universe – to decide.

"Maybs I'll get a signif sentence.
That totes depends on the jury."

Mensh: *mention*

In Yiddish, a *mensch* is a person possessed of admirable characteristics, such as fortitude, firmness of purpose, and other extremely-rare-in-real-life qualities you might expect to find attributed to the hero of a windswept romantic novel. But in certain linguistically tits-up pockets of the internet, largely populated by people who use emoticons to react to news and events, *mensh* is short for *mention*.

"How was I to know?
He didn't mensh having a wife..."

Morto: *mortified, mortifying*

In Esperanto, this means "death", but for Totes Ridicheads, it's the last not-quite-a-word in pure embarrassment. *Morto* was grown in a meth lab using DNA from the verb *mortified*, and tends to ripple through cyberspace like a tsunami if James Franco hosts the Oscars or Lindsay Lohan makes a new film. (It's all been downhill since *Mean Girls*, Linds.)

"She meant to text the photo to her boyfriend, but accidentally sent it to her dad! She was abso morto."

Natch: *natural, naturally*

An abbrev so old it pre-dates the existence of iPods and Jennifer Lawrence, *natch* rose to prominence in the early 1990s, when stoned Californian surfer types (think Brad Pitt in *True Romance*, or Patrick "Nobody Puts Baby in the Corner" Swayze circa *Point Break*) and people fond of extensively quoting Beavis and Butt-head would say it instead of *naturally*. Once something of a lone ugly duckling in the slang world, *natch* is now a bona fide original in a sea of totes tradge imitators.

"Natch we all follow Justin Bieber on Twitter."

Nause: *to nauseate or annoy; someone who does this*

If you tweet pointless, witless dross about the minutiae of your life approximately once every three seconds, at least some of your followers will consider you a *nause* – someone so irritating that they turn people's stomachs.

A *nause* might do things like read a Dan Brown book in public without feeling remotely self-conscious; fill their status updates with #humblebrags about how totes amaze their life is; or suddenly get "tired" and go home when it's their turn to buy a round of drinks.

"My mom can be such a nause sometimes.
The things that woman comes out with!"

Neiths: *neither*

Way back through the turbulent sands of time, before Tumblr or wi-fi even existed, Neith was an Egyptian mother goddess who nursed baby crocodiles and wove baskets. Because Egyptian mythology was so progressive that all women had to be domesticated, even if they were gods.

Be that as it may, the almighty Neith would no doubt be less than thrilled to learn that her name has latterly been taken in vain, had an s slapped on its tail-end, and is now totes-ridic speak for *neither*. But in a fast-paced digital world where neither the English language nor HBO's desire for the internet's populace to refrain from illegally downloading the shit out of *Game of Thrones* are sacred, what chance do pre-Biblical deities have?

"You're not going?
Yeah, me neiths."

Nekkid: *naked*

Nekkid achieves the remarkable feat of making nudity sound really annoying, rather than something that 90 percent of all internet usage is devoted to the viewing of. If you asked a toddler or someone tripping their nuts off on ketamine to spell the word that best describes what Michael Fassbender so often gets onscreen, this is what they'd write.

Offering neither abbreviation nor simplification, *nekkid* is a reversion to the primordial sludge from which *naked* finally emerged. On social media, it's what people want to look at and look good as; it is the state in which we all entered this world and usually enter the shower; it is the source of much of humankind's desire and despair.

If ever Appletinis and crushing loneliness drive you to send someone a *nekkid* picture of yourself, don't, whatever you do, embark upon a political career. This is a well-travelled path – one which inevitably ends with the individual in question becoming the *National Enquirer*'s bitch-slave.

"When I want a guy to love and respect me for who I am, I just get nekkid."

Nevs: *never*

Like pride, *nevs* comes before a fall. Because, all too often, when someone says they're *nevs* going to do something again – like sleep with that insensitive ass-hat who doesn't return their calls, take any more shit from their boss, or eat unethically sourced meat – before you know it, they're flat on their back in that sock-scented bedroom, sending pleading late-night emails on their BlackBerry and inhaling a Big Mac as though it were oxygen.

If the adverb *never* were an adolescent girl going through a not entirely convincing phase of teenage rebellion, she would be *nevs* – more likely, for example, to spite her mother by turning vegetarian, rather than doing anything properly hardcore like going to a three-day rave with her new, 30-year-old, ex-convict boyfriend.

"Seize the day, babes. It's now or nevs."

Obnox: *obnoxious*

Obnox. As in obnoxious. As in odious, horrible, extremely unpleasant –
like Simon Cowell pantomime-scowling from behind the immobile wall
of Botox that used to be his forehead, or Reese Witherspoon trying to
dissuade a police officer from arresting her after "one too many" glasses
of wine, or pretty much anyone, ever, on cocaine.

*"I tweeted asking if she wanted to come and
she was like, 'Whevs.' She's being totes obnox.
She's, like, an obnoxy moron."*

Obsesh: *obsessed, obsession*

If you've ever experienced the terrible joy of becoming unhealthily fixated
on a song, food, film, book, app or person, you know what it is to revel
in the throes of an *obsesh* – which is how overenthusiastic smartphone-
fingerers say *obsession* in the Snapchat age.

Common teenage *obseshes* include JBiebs, HStyles, and that one
from Union J who looks like he has fillers in his cheeks despite barely
having passed through puberty. Common adult *obseshes* include iPhones,
infidelity and glacially-paced Scandinavian crime dramas. *Obseshes* liable
to take hold irrespective of the *obseshee's* age include Khaleesi from
Game of Thrones, Angry Birds and retweeting dog gifs.

"Hmm. Hummingbird cupcakes are totes my new obsesh."

Obvs: *obvious, obviously*

Derived from the adjective *obvious*. When something goes without saying, but still needs to be remarked upon – like Keanu Reeves's fundamental inability to act, or *Downton Abbey*'s Lady Mary and Matthew Crawley having the fizzing sexual chemistry of two mouldy tea bags – it will be given the *obvs* treatment.

"Believe me, the last thing I want to do is hurt him, but obvs it's still on the list."

Omish: *omit, omitted, omission*

This looks kind of like a misspelling of Amish, and, in some cases, that's probably what it is. But other times, it's a swishy-tailed disciple of *omit* or *omission*. We've all been there: mercilessly *omished* from the coolest clique in school, from the wedding guest-list, from the relative's will, from the group invite to the art-deco villa in southern Spain. Not being included can be painful and alienating, but sometimes it's a blessing in disguise.

After all, the coolest clique in school usually grow up to have sales jobs and unattractive children. There wasn't even a free bar at that wedding (*and* it rained). Your life wouldn't really have improved if you'd inherited an antique grandfather clock. And they all spent most of that Spanish holiday shitting their guts out after eating dodgy squid on the second night. Life, oh life.

"I can't believe she said that about you!
I'm totes gonna omish her from the party invites."

Partics: *particular, particularly*

If you're the fussy type, you may spend a lot of time looking for *particular* things – a perfectly mixed Bloody Mary; an item of clothing that conveys the true depths of your individuality and free spiritedness; friends whose dinner-table conversation doesn't make you think that Facebook is, in fact, a more than adequate substitute for human interaction.

Thanks to the crushing inevitability of that hyper-modern purgatory otherwise known as the internet, *particular* or *particularly* have been divested of a few vowels and are now *partics*. As in:

"No, you're totes not listening. ALL of your outfit is horrible – that skirt in partics."

Perf: *perfect, perfectly*

If you've arranged a mutually agreeable time to meet friends for cocktails, laid eyes upon a jacket you just can't live without, or gazed approvingly at a stranger's arse on public transport, you may well find cause to utter a breathless *perf*. Like *perfect*, but with fewer letters and less hope, *perf* is notably popular with individuals who've turned the quiet annihilation of other people's self-esteem into an art-form.

"Did you see the Facebook photo of Yvonne passed out on the toilet at Michael's party? That was too perf."

Plezh: *pleasure*

Pleasure is something timid virgins got from reading novels in dusty drawing rooms during the 1800s. *Plezh* is what knowing pop-culture tech-whores get from gorging on pizza and frozen margaritas while tweeting the funniest passages of *Fifty Shades of Grey* and/or tongue-in-cheek commentary about Taylor Swift's love life – possibly with a Ryan Gosling Netflix marathon playing in the background. The abbrev also provides a handy way of feigning politeness.

"Oh, it's my plezh, you're totes welcome."

Presh: *precious*

Like adorbs, *presh* is favoured by Twitter-centric adolescents and twentysomethings as a means of labelling something cute – be it a kitten, a handbag, a kitten in a handbag, or a man who makes them think PG-13 thoughts. (A piece of these people's hearts died forever the day Zac Efron started making the move into "grown-up" films with plots that revolve around Nicole Kidman weeing on him, rather than tweengasmic homages to Vanessa Hudgens's auto-tuned singing voice.)

"He is totes presh. I so would."

Probs: *probably, problems*

It can mean one of two things, this abbrev. Either that which Jay-Z famously rapped about having 99 of (*problems*). Or what you say when someone asks if you'll be out later, and you know there's a good chance you'll just stay in, eat cereal and Facebook-stalk people you think might sleep with you if enough alcohol was involved, but you want to keep your options – such as they are – open (*probably*).

Two random sentences plucked from a Twitter search illustrate this divide:

- "I can't stand being around people with attitude probs." (Translation: "My unhappy childhood means I'll spend the rest of my life starting fights with total strangers.")
- "Probs won't make it through the whole day without crying lol." (Translation: "Please, somebody – ANYBODY – ask me if I'm okay. Twitter needs to hear about my misery in detail, but I can't just tweet it apropos of nothing because that would be weird.")

Either way, it goes without saying that insecurity and despair are the real grease on the internet's wheels. (And porn, obvs.)

"I got 99 probs but ridic ain't one."

Rando: *random person*

Ah, *randos*, they're everywhere. The friends you haven't met. Or, more commonly, the overenthusiastic drunks whose friend requests you accept on Facebook but who you know you'll never see again. There will usually be at least one or two who've tagged along when you all go back to someone's house after a club. "Who do you know here? No one? Oh." If they're a good *rando*, they'll share their drug stash and start regaling you with risqué insider stories about celebrities they've encountered. If they're a bad *rando*, they'll drink the last of the vodka and steal money from the master bedroom.

"No one even knew who he was.
He just showed up, a total rando."

Redonk: *ridiculous*

In the beginning, there was only *ridiculous*. As time passed, penicillin was invented, man walked on the moon, and Twitter revolutionised the way we communicate by allowing people to give each other minute-by-minute updates about how bored they are at work. In this progressive, forward-thinking global climate, *ridiculous* begat *redonkulous*, which later begat *redonk*.

"Ugh, he rented the Swedish version of The Girl with the Dragon Tattoo *by mistake. He's being totes redonk if he thinks I'm sitting through two hours of subtitles."*

Remembs: *remember*

The thing no one can ever do the morning after the night before. "Remembs using your credit card to buy a round for the whole bar?" Er… "Remembs when you vommed into your wine glass?" Not… really… "Remembs performing a full-length, a cappella rendition of 'Bad Romance' for that homeless guy outside Burger King even though he offered *you* money to stop?" And so on and so forth.

Usually, these gaping memory blanks are a defence mechanism on the part of your ever-vulnerable ego – or else a regrettable testament to the fact that you can no longer match your 22-year-old self drink for drink. But whatevs, very little of the average individual's life is actually worth remembering anyway.

Obviously you should consign any Oscar wins and the births of your children to the reinforced steel citadel of your innermost memory banks, but apart from that? The reason you can never recall all the thousands of hours you've wasted standing in line at the supermarket or staring dead-eyed at a computer screen is because being able to revisit the barrage of unutterable tedium that makes up most of your existence in any real detail would drive you absolutely bat-shit crazy.

"Just remembs one thing: never, ever feed them after midnight."

Ridic: *ridiculous*

On the morally bereft streets of Twitter, *ridic* is one of the biggest, baddest muthafuckas out there, second-in-command only to *totes*, who seized power in a bloody coup at the turn of the twecade (Twitter decade).

Nonetheless, *ridic* still enjoys a lot of clout. Its meals and women come free of charge wherever it goes, and it appears on Twitter and Facebook an average of six times a minute. (Disclaimer: data may be totes inaccs.) It used to be – like, obvsballs – *ridiculous*, but, as is so often the case, fame changed it, it stopped returning its friends' calls and, well, now it's simply *ridic*.

"He sleeps with his BlackBerry IN his hand. This is getting ridic."

Rubs: *rubbish*

Not a suspect variety of sensual massage that a middle-aged man with an above-averagely hairy back might journey to Thailand to receive, but an abbrev of *rubbish*. When you don't get recalled for that second interview, have your heart pulverized by a total shit who just won't commit, or max out your credit card shopping on Amazon whilst inebriated, friends may offer a consolatory, "Aw, babes, that's rubs."

"That Carly Rae Jepsen single is totes rubs."

Selfie: *self-portrait*

If, like everyone else, your fragile self-esteem is measured in Facebook likes, and the degree of self-loathing you feel at any given time is directly related to how many retweets your Instagrammed photographs of sunsets receive, then you'll probably already know the pleasures and pains of the *selfie* (from the ye olde English, *self-portrait*).

Back in the dark age of the "MySpace pose", these photos were usually taken from above with a pixelation-prone camera phone, all the better to highlight those sucked-in cheeks and emo fringes. Now, thanks to the fact that people fancy their iPhones almost as much as themselves – and the forgiving nature of Instagram's ever-popular Lo-Fi filter (better than any Vaseline lens) – the modern *selfie* commonly involves mirrors, mood lighting, partial nudity and a "Blue Steel" gaze thoughtfully averted from the device you're pointing at yourself.

"Ugh, don't use that selfie on your OkCupid profile – you totes look like a dick."

Sesh: *session*

A *sesh* is a versatile creature: you can have a work sesh, gym sesh, sex sesh, pizza-and-DVD sesh, cleaning sesh, shopping sesh, internet sesh, prescription-meds sesh, bong sesh, booze sesh, bitch sesh (like a bitch fest, but slightly less cruel). The list goes on.

"I'm never more flexible than I am after a yoga sesh."

Shamazing: *amazing*

Shamazing owes its existence to former Pussycat Doll and linguistic trailblazer Nicole Scherzinger, who casually dropped it into the mix while serving as a judge on *The X Factor*. Somewhat predictably, the internet was all over that shit like a rash, and the word – according to Nicole, a compound of *shazam* and *amazing* – caught on. Along the way, another even more annoying variant emerged: *shamazeballs*. (But people generally only use that when they secretly want strangers to do them physical harm.)

"That performance was shamazing!"

Signif: *significant*

Signif moments in human history include the Renaissance, the birth of Tom Cruise, the fall of the Berlin Wall, and Janet Jackson's Super Bowl nip slip. *Signif* moments in your life include the first time you let another human being feel you up, moved out of your parents' house, drank so much that you projectile vomited on a stranger, and your conclusive realisation that most adults have absolutely no idea what they're doing either.

"Do you think it's signif that he always showers straight afterwards?"

Soz: *sorry*

It is a truth universally acknowledged that when people say *sorry*, they often don't really mean it, but are merely paying lip-service to good manners, conventional morality, and all the other tedious hoops one is required to jump through in order to be perceived as a functional member of society.

If someone apologises by saying *soz*, however, they're essentially rolling their eyes, playing with their hair, idly chewing gum, and probably planning to raise two fingers in your direction the moment your back is turned. Further evidence of this abbreviation's pathological insincerity can be seen in the fact that any given *soz* hurled into the void of Twitter or Facebook is statistically highly likely to be preceded or followed by a *lol*. For example, "Sum1 just dropped there iPhone on the train track LOL soz," or: "Never tidying my room again. Soz mum lol."

Soz is *sorry* stripped of its eloquence, presentability and long-term job prospects. It will most likely die in the gutter, shaking its fist at the sky and ranting about how it coulda been a contender. Frankly, it's inadvisable to use *soz* in any context other than when you're writing a tweet or text and are on the verge of tearing your character limit a new arsehole. (And even then, you should probably hate yourself for it. Soz.)

"Er, yeah. It was me who spilled beer on your laptop while looking at porn. Soz."

Spectac: *spectacular*

The Great Wall of China as seen from space, the infinitesimal majesty of the aurora borealis, the box-office receipts of the *Twilight* films, Madonna's ego. Such wonders, be they manmade or naturally occurring, are *spectac – spectacular*.

"He was so drunk that he started throwing things and crying about how his father never really loved him. It was spectac."

Spesh: *special*

All babies are *spesh* – that is, *special*. Perfect, unblighted by the world's moral dissolution, destined for great things. Well, *possibly* destined for great things. In much the same way that the accused are innocent until proven guilty, babies are potential future geniuses until proven thick as two short planks.

But time is cruel, and *spesh* babies frequently grow up to become nondescript adults. We may all be unique snowflakes, but unless you're an especially wealthy, famous or influential snowflake – well, in this frenzied capitalist global nightmare, the ball's not exactly in your corner.

"I'm totes saving my virginity for that spesh someone. ROFL! LOL! LULZ! Yeah, right."

Suspish: *suspicious, suspiciously*

Your spouse is acting *suspish* – that is to say, *suspiciously*, which means they're probably having an affair. WTF! What do you do? Sure, you could confront him/her, and have a frank, mature discussion about your apparently doomed relationship, addressing practical matters – like who'll get custody of the joint Netflix account when you go your separate ways.

Or you could go through their texts, hack their email account, and scrutinize their Facebook and Twitter messages in search of cold, hard, sexually active proof of this most ultimate of betrayals. Then post compromising photos of them to a revenge-porn site. They'll either be humiliated, or become a media personality, *à la* Kim Kardashian. Either way, they'll learn a valuable lesson, which is: never become emotionally attached to a man, woman, beast or child.

"He hasn't got drunk and pestered me for sex for nearly five days. It's totes suspish."

Swag: *style, appearance*

In the 1960s, *swag* was apparently coined as code for "secretly we are gay". In the 2010s, it's either a way of complimenting an individual's style ("He's totes got swag"), or, more generally, one of those online catchphrases that people – especially teenagers – will include in literally any sentence. For example: "Totes cheated on that test, SWAG." "Dude, you're deffo a swaginator." "So high right now. SWAG!" "She's so swag I'm havin' swag-gasms." "Obvs just turned my swag on." "Swag, there are gherkins in my burger."

To paraphrase Homer Simpson: children are the future, unless we stop them now.

"You've got amazeballs levels of swag happening."

Terrif: *terrific*

Terrific, a word that conjures images of gout-faced aristocrats giving the thumbs up as their purebred horse races across the finish line, has been shorn of its winter fur, pumped full of triple-shot lattes, and is single'n'ready to mingle. It's *terrif*.

On the totes-ridic scale of enthusiastic OMG-ness, *terrif* isn't quite up there with *amazeballs* or *brill*, but dwells somewhere in the hinterland above *marv*. It's what you might say if, for example, your friend received a promotion at a shit-hot media startup while you were unemployed and surviving on ramen noodles. "Wow, that's terrif." You're happy for them, but it's the resentful kind of happy. You're only human, after all.

"You're giving up your job to retrain as a massage therapist? That's, um, terrif."

Togeths: *together*

When two young people want to commit to each other online after a prolonged period (i.e. a week) of twirting that progressed to sexting that progressed to Skyping that progressed to "in a relationship with" on Facebook – more binding, in its way, than accidental pregnancy or cohabitation – they might well type: "We'll be togeths forevs." Meaning that they'll be together, forever, in electric dreams. Just like Philip Oakey's deathless 1984 masterpiece promised.

"I was wondering if you wanted to go to prom togeths?"

Tomaz: *tomorrow*

The Twitter ne'er-do-well's term for *tomorrow*, that gilded fantasy realm in which you always imagine yourself getting a better job, finding butterfly-stomached true love, starting your voice-of-a-generation novel, or simply attending one of the Pilates classes you booked on Groupon back in 2010. (And those have long since expired. Yes, bad things *do* happen to good people.)

When not being used to make plans of the "I'll you see you tomaz at 8:30" variety, this abbrev, like the Merriam-Webster-approved word it was ripped bodily from, is an excuse, a get-out-of-jail-free card, a talisman we wave at the world in a futile attempt to ward off the po-faced spectre of our regrets, broken promises and lack of accomplishments. You'll call her *tomaz*, you'll trim the hedge *tomaz*, you swear you'll start the diet *tomaz* – etcetera. Until one day, it's too late and you die regretting everything, pleading to the cruel gods above for more time. Which is something to look forward to.

"I'm going to sort my life out tomaz, deffo."

Totes: *totally*

Totes is essentially the President of the United Abbreviations; the Abraham Lincoln of internet slang. When Hollywood finally comes to tell the *totes* story, the abbrev will be portrayed by Daniel Day-Lewis, who'll subsequently accept his nineteenth best actor Oscar by delivering a one-word speech: "MEGALOLZ."

But seriously, during the Twitter Revolution of 2008, the adverb *totally* was one of the first words to die for its beliefs, approaching the guillotine with dignity and resolve, willing to sacrifice itself in the name of progress and mankind's ability to save a few precious seconds here and there whilst typing. When they pulled its twitching head out of the basket, that head was *totes*.

Teenage girls love *totes*, as do the online multitudes who aren't teenage girls but find it amusing to "ironically" talk or tweet like teenage girls. It's a most versatile abbrev that can rise to many occasions: you'll *totes* be there, you *totes* love it, you *totes* hate him *and* that skanky whore he's been running around with, you'll *totes* be BFFs until the apocalypse comes (an extinction-level event possibly to be heralded by one of Russell Crowe's exquisitely voiced solos from *Les Mis*).

"Her profile pic is totes fugly."

Tradge: *tragic*

Slang-wise, *tragic* is less likely to describe something steeped in genuine distress or sorrow than an event/action/thing that is perceived as uncool, desperate, or otherwise failed and reprehensible – like bootcut jeans, MySpace, or the eyeball-gouging Photoshop holocaust of the now-legendary *Sex and the City 2* poster. It is often shortened – if only phonetically, which is a bit of an abbrev fail – to *tradge*.

"He sent me like a million private messages, begging me to go out with him. It was totes tradge."

Twerk: *to work it*

If you've ever taken to the dancefloor after six rum-and-cokes and some disco dust of questionable provenance and felt the bass line from "Crazy in Love" throbbing through the tips of your fingers to the fleshy curve of your rear-end, chances are that you'll have already found cause to twerk it.

To *twerk* means, in essence, to shake yo' ass so hard you inject new meaning into the term "bootylicious" – like so much silicon into a butt cheek. As is the case with most sexually suggestive dance moves, *twerking* is a great way of getting people to like you for who you are.

"That girl is totes twerkin' it. I shall make her my wife."

Unforch: *unfortunate, unfortunately*

If *unfortunate* and *unfortunately* are the kind of suit-wearing, child-rearing, mortgage-paying office drones whose idea of a racy weekend involves a bottle of sauvignon blanc and the *Breaking Bad* box set, *unforch* is the intermittently employed college drop-out from next door, who breakfasts on bongs, thinks grammar is located somewhere in Germany, and swears by the pull-out technique as a legitimate method of contraception.

"Unforch we can't make it. He's already too drunk to drive."

Vacay: *vacation*

Typically involving – but not limited to – sun, sea, sand and sexiness, a *vacay* is your two-week reward for making it through the other fifty weeks of the year without having a nervous breakdown. If this doesn't *quite* seem like a fair trade-off, that's because it isn't. But society still has a long way to go.

You'll eat, swim, read, relax. The sun will tan you a healthy golden brown, until you find it hard to believe that you spend most of your life nurturing a vitamin D deficiency under grey office strip-lighting. You'll get vague withdrawal symptoms from the lack of regular internet access. You'll order another cocktail elaborately decorated with pineapple slices and miniature umbrellas. You'll slather on a third layer of factor 25 sunscreen, and reflect upon life's infinite possibilities. Then, just before you board the plane back to reality, a small part of you will die forever.

"If I don't have a vacay soon this place is going to break me."

Vocab: *vocabulary*

Depending on how you use it, the internet can either expand or eradicate your *vocab*. Spend too much time communicating via Twitter and Facebook comment threads, and you're liable to start saying things like *totes* and *whevs* IRL ("in real life", feel it). If this happens, people will either think you're a hipster ironist, a dick, or both. But spend too little time Twacebooking, and you'll have no idea what the hipster ironists who've somehow infiltrated your social circle are on about when they start referring to "selfiesteem" (taking selfies with low self-esteem) or "procrastinhating" (procrastinating because you dislike the person who would benefit from action being taken).

"He has the vocab of a stoned badger. He's totes boring."

Whatevs: *whatever*

"Whateverrrr" was the defining catchphrase of mid-'90s adolescence, and now reliably invokes a roll call of the era's better-known bored youths: Bart Simpson, Cher Horowitz from *Clueless*, Angela Chase from *My So-Called Life*, and, er, Beavis and Butt-head. *Whatevs* is the illogical progression of that blasé, dismissive sentiment, sometimes shortened even further by zeitgeist-chasers to *whevs*.

You say it to your parents, to your teachers, to your friends, to the bartender who refuses to serve you without ID. You don't care, not really. You don't need their money, their rules, their companionship, their alcohol. Welcome to a town named Couldn't Give A Fuck. Population: you.

"He was all, 'I don't even like you enough to put up with this shit.' And I was all, 'Whatevs.'"

Yolo: *you only live once*

Not twice, as certain James Bond films claim. Not nine times, as cats, erm, don't. Not eternally, as some of the less imaginative religions would would have us believe. But once. So make the most of it: speak truthfully, live passionately, follow your dreams even in the vengeful, crushing face of reality. Hell, drink full fat Coke and treat yourself to the odd bucket of fried chicken if you feel like it. Go home with that stranger. Break up with that douchebag. Tell your friend what you *really* think of his new haircut. React honestly to the news of your number-one drinking partner's pregnancy. Life is short, brutal, and quite often boring. But you only get to do it once.

"C'mon, just try a little bit, stop being so lame. Yolo, y'know?"

Yoozh: *usual, usually*

As with *usual*, its less fashionable predecessor, *yoozh* is frequently used to articulate the pervading sense of monotony and futility that pulses through modern life like blood through a depressed teenager's veins – an existential dread well documented in the films of Lars von Trier, the novels (and Twitter feed) of Bret Easton Ellis, and the songs of One Direction. (See also: *the boozual*, used when ordering a drink at your regular watering hole.)

"This Friday I'm gonna get some takeout, have a bath, watch America's Next Top Model – the yoozh."

TOTES
RIDIC
ULARITY

MOVIES · POP ART
PETS · VINTAGE

King Kong (1933)

The Wizard of Oz (1939)

The Seven Year Itch (1955)

The Godfather (1972)

Jaws (1975)

The Shining (1980)

Indiana Jones and the Temple of Doom (1984)

Edward Scissorhands (1990)

Forrest Gump (1994)

Pulp Fiction (1994)

Toy Story (1995)

Titanic (1997)

The Lord of the Rings: The Two Towers (2002)

Twilight (2008)

Star Trek: Into Darkness (2013)

It's totes ridic that *her* blog became a book when mine gets twice as many unique visitors each week. #Whatevs

Hun, there's obvs no point in paying for gym membs if you're never gonna use it.

TWIST

ORICAL

ROMANCE

IF HISTORY AND LITERATURE'S

FAMOUS COUPLES WERE ON TWITTER…

Adam and Eve
(circa the
Dawn of Mankind)

@TheOriginalAdam

@Eve Wow! Ur like me, but nicer 2 look at. I never thought sumthin made from 1 of my ribs could make me feel so, um, expectant.

@Eve

@TheOriginalAdam Thnx. U'd think we'd be totes self-conscious about standing here in the buff, but no. #SoWeird #PreKnowledge

@TheOriginalAdam

@Eve Before I forget: whatever you do, DON'T eat any of the fruit from that tree. Or we'll both be in cray-cray trouble.

@Eve

@TheOriginalAdam Er, OK. Deets?

@TheOriginalAdam

@Eve The landlord, @God, is a nice guy but *whispers* a bit of a control freak.

@Eve

@TheOriginalAdam Ah, say no more. I totes know the type, lol.

@NoOneSuspectsTheSerpent

@Eve Babes, you should deffo try the totes forbids fruit. It's better than 2-4-1 cocktails, sexting and shoes COMBINED. #GetYourSinOn

@Eve

@NoOneSuspectsTheSerpent Totes, you seem trustworthy. *bites* OMG, this is gorge. Why is the good stuff always bad for you? #GottaStartADiet

@TheOriginalAdam

@Eve YOU ATE THE FRUIT!!!!!! @God IS GONNA GO APESHIT. THIS IS TOTES RIDIC!!!

@Eve

@TheOriginalAdam Why does the only potential boyf in existence have to be so uptight? Chillax, try some. It's delish. A bit like chicken.

@TheOriginalAdam

@Eve O to the M to the G. It really is.

@God

Sigh I've obvs created idiots. @TheOriginalAdam @Eve U R both hereby cast out of paradise for ALL ETERNITY. #Rejected

@TheOriginalAdam

Great. We've condemned humanity to centuries of Twitter, hangovers, the agony of childbirth and hatred of our own naked bodies. #TheFall

@Eve

@TheOriginalAdam Babes, it's not all bad. Look, I've made a totes presh bikini from fig leaves. #SelfSufficient #IAmWoman

King Henry VIII and Anne Boleyn

(1533)

@HailKingHenry8
@AnneBoleyn1522 U R hot, have fiiiiiine hips and, verily, will totes bear me the son I need to chillax on the throne after I tweet my last.

@AnneBoleyn1522
@HailKingHenry8 Flattery, sire, will get U everywhere. Every other woman in this court is gonna be WELL JEL!!!

@HailKingHenry8
@AnneBoleyn1522 My preve marriage is totes annulled. #Henry4Anne4Eva #UrHereToBearASonAndHeir

@AnneBoleyn1522
@HailKingHenry8 I deffo WILL produce a male heir, but, like, I'm not gonna lose my head over it. Back off @JaneSeymour #NoMoreWivesAfterMe

Romeo and Juliet

@JulietCaps
Oh Romeo, my ovaries LITERALLY exploded. But it makes me totes emosh that my only love has sprung from my only hate. #Typical

@Romeo_Montague
@JulietCaps Down here! I think ur srsly gorge 2 and, luckily for us, teenage lust lasts forever and transcends everything – even generations of hate. #LetsGetMarried

@JulietCaps
@Romeo_Montague You were spying on my balcony?
#TotesInappropes But whatevs, I can't turn 17 and be SINGLE, so I accept.

@Romeo_Montague
@JulietCaps Secret weddings FTW. #TotesGettingLaid

@JulietCaps
@Romeo_Montague There is no way that youthful hubris and industrial-strength sleeping pills can ever backfire. #Consummated

@WillShakespeare
As you know, R&J are dead now. But their memory will live on for hundreds of years – largely in the minds of teenagers resentfully cramming for exams. #soz

Robin Hood and Maid Marian

(circa 1600)

@MaidMarian
@RHoodOutlaw Your Sherwood Forest version of the Ewok Village is adorbs. BTW, can u smell that?

@RHoodOutlaw
@MaidMarian Er, yeah. The thing is, I've been living in the woods 4 sum months and baths are cray-cray diffs 2 come by.

@MaidMarian
@RHoodOutlaw Gross.

@RHoodOutlaw
@MaidMarian BUT @TheMerryMen just intercepted the @SheriffOfNotts's Domino's Pizza Meal Deal if ur hungry?

@MaidMarian
@RHoodOutlaw Shldn't u like, give that 2 the poor?

@RHoodOutlaw
@MaidMarian We'll obvs save them sum slices.

@LittleJohn
@RHoodOutlaw Whatevs. I'm staaaaaaaaaaaaaaaarvin. #RobFromTheRichAndFeedYOURSELF

@MaidMarian
@RHoodOutlaw Perf. Can we listen 2 that Bryan Adams song again? #EverythingIDoIDoItForYou

@RHoodOutlaw
@MaidMarian FML…

Antony and Cleopatra

@MarkAntonyRulesOK
Octavia is adorbs. But no other hotties R as hot as Cleopatra.
#LoveHer #WomanOfMyHeart

@LTEnorbarbus
Totes. Facebook cannot wither her. Nor Twitter stale her infinite variety.

@CleopatraCominAtcha
@MarkAntonyRulesOK Yeah Octavia's OK… If u like short-arsed
women with crap hair and ZERO personality. #Fuming

@MarkAntonyRulesOK
@CleopatraCominAtcha Aw, babe, how about if we rule Rome
together? Will that make you feel better?!

@CleopatraCominAtcha
@MarkAntonyRulesOK Er, obvs. #Ants&CleoFTW

@MarkAntonyRulesOK
@CleopatraCominAtcha Us bein able to tweet at each other =
eliminates most of Shakespeare's convoluted plot. #NoTragedyHere

@CleopatraCominAtcha
@MarkAntonyRulesOK Um, awkward. I kinda entered into this
relationship on the understanding that U'd die in my arms…

@MarkAntonyRulesOK
@CleopatraCominAtcha Anything for Cleo… *dies by own hand*

@CleopatraCominAtcha
@MarkAntonyRulesOK Babes, I'll join U as soon as I locate the poison
of an asp. Currently lookin for 1 on eBay. #BiddingWar

Napoleon and Josephine

@NapolesBonz
@JPheneBeau I am full of U. Your gorge profile pic and last evening's wine-addled sexting has left me cray-cray in lurrrrrrve.

@NapolesBonz
@JPheneBeau Mio dolce amor, I abso abandon myself to the profound emosh that totes masters me. Your kisses deffo burn my blood. U R my obsesh.

@NapolesBonz
@JPheneBeau Um, u nevs reply to my #sexytweets and there R rumors that ur cheating on me with half the French court.

@NapolesBonz
@JPheneBeau FFS, I'M AT WAR you frigid ice queen. A little bit of twirting shouldn't be beyond you.

@JPheneBeau
@NapolesBonz Tbf you are *quite* a bit younger than me. Not to mention away ALL the time. A woman has needs. #Yolo

@NapolesBonz
@JPheneBeau You vile, beastly slutbag. I'm totes going to have as many cray-cray hot affairs as I can orchestrate. #Syphilis #Divorce

@JPheneBeau
@NapolesBonz Babes, forgive me. My Twitter obvs got hacked. I'd NEVER betray your love and trust… or your money and status.

Elizabeth Bennet and Mr Darcy
Pride and Prejudice

(1813)

@lizzybennet93
@thedarcinator Srsly, Uve been a real dick recently an it's totes ridic that you made my sis miserable & treated Mr Wickham that way.

@thedarcinator
@lizzybennet93 Bbz, Ur sis wanted Bingley for his cash. Wickham spunked his fortune away gamblin an tried to wed MY lil sis to get her money.

@lizzybennet93
@thedarcinator WTF?! Wickham is a shit. I'm totes seeing u in a diffs light Darcy.

@thedarcinator
@lizzybennet93 Lets stop playin games. I think ur gorge an I'm in possession of a fortune – will u marry me?

@lizzybennet93
@thedarcinator OMG YES!!!!!!!!!!! BTW, Colin Firth in a wet shirt FTW.
134 Retweets

Scarlett O'Hara and Rhett Butler
Gone with the Wind

@scarlettohara
I'm feelin crappy. Widowed, preggers, married again, preggers again, the civil war. And u know who keeps messin with my head. #NamingNoNames

@rhettbutlerisaplaya
@scarlettohara If ur gonna say it say it to my face. What knd of wife r u? Evry1 knows about u and Ashley. It's totes inapropes.

@scarlettohara
@rhettbutlerisaplaya Whatevs, Rhett. Maybe u shld ave another drink, right? Thats all u eva do. It's separate beds from now on. #HateUSoMuch

@rhettbutlerisaplaya
@scarlettohara Yeah, separate beds unless uve been drinkin. #ShesEasy... Aw, babe, u an me could've been happy. I luv'd u. I know u.

@scarlettohara
@rhettbutlerisaplaya Happy? Thnx to u Im pregnant AGAIN. Do I want it tho? No!!!

@rhettbutlerisaplaya
@scarlettohara Im so drunk. Bonnie's dead. Everything's gone. It's over. Im goin back 2 the south...

@scarlettohara
@rhettbutlerisaplaya Rhett!!! Where will I go? What will I do?!?!

@rhettbutlerisaplaya
@scarlettohara Frankly, my dear, I dont give a damn. An Im deactivatin my Twitter.

Sid Vicious
and Nancy Spungen

@SidVish77
@NancyLauraSpungen Maybe it's the smack talkin, but ur lookin totes presh Nance. Ur makin me MIND about the bollocks, lol.

@NancyLauraSpungen
@SidVish77 It was deffo the smack talkin when you did that Frank Sinatra cover, babe…

@SidVish77
@NancyLauraSpungen Whatevs, just text the dealer, yeah? Ur less irritating when I'm off my tits.

@NancyLauraSpungen
@SidVish77 Ur a dick. But @JohnnyRotten wasn't interested. Let's just go back to the #ChelseaHotel. What's the worst that could happen?

@SidVish77
@NancyLauraSpungen The worst? Um, I dunno – a murder/suicide type thing?

@JohnnyRotten
@SidVish77 @NancyLauraSpungen Ever get the feeling U've been cheated?

Published by Plexus Publishing Ltd
25 Mallinson Road
London SW11 1BW
www.plexusbooks.com

British Library Cataloguing in Publication Data
A catalogue record for this book is available
from the British Library

ISBN-13: 978-0-85965-511-8

Text by Tom Branton
Cover and book design by Coco Wake-Porter
Printed in China on behalf of Latitude Press Ltd
by WKT Company Ltd

Acknowledgements

We would like to thank Mateja Osonjacki
and Alex Chapman for alerting us to the totes
ridic phenomenon, Coco Wake-Porter for
the idea of creating a book about it and her
design, and Pepe Balderrama for coming up
with the title. But, most importantly, thanks to
Tom Branton for writing the text and creating
this totes amaze book. Thanks also to Laura
Slater and Laura Coulman for their insight,
suggestions and feedback.

We'd also like to thank the following
agencies for providing pictures: Lynea/
Shutterstock; Moviestore Collection/ Rex
Features; Everett Collection/ Rex Features;
20th C.Fox/ Everett/ Rex Features; SNAP/
Rex Features; lavitrei/ Shutterstock; CSA
Images/ Mod Art Collection/ Vetta/ Getty
Images; Jmcdermottillo/ Shutterstock; CSA
Images/ Mod Art Collection/ Getty Images;
Jacquie Boyd/ Ikon Images/ Getty Images;
SaulHerrera/ iStock Vectors/ iStockphoto;
jameslee1/ iStock Vectors/ iStockphoto;
tatarnikova/ iStock Vectors/ iStockphoto;
CSA Images/ Mod Art Collection/ Getty
Images; LeeDaniels/ iStock Vectors/
iStockphoto; Evan Kafka/ Stone/ Getty;
Wallace Garrison/ Photographer's Choice
RF/ Getty Images; Fabrizio Cacciatore/
Photolibrary/ Getty Images; Andrew Bret
Wallis/ Stockbyte/ Getty Images; Harriet
Paine/ age footstock/ Getty Images; Zoran
Milich/ Photonica/ Getty Images; Whitney
Johnson/ Flickr Select/ Getty Images; Joel
Sartore/ National Geographic/ Getty Images;
Lori Adamski Peek/ Photographer's Choice/
Getty Images; Gandee Vasan/ Riser/Getty
Images; Genevieve Morrison/ Flickr/ Getty
Images; Pai-Shih Lee/ Flickr/ Getty Images;
GK Hart/ Vikki Hart/ Taxi/ Getty Images;
LeoCH Studio/ Flickr Select/ Getty Images;
Paula Daniëlse/ Flickr Select/ Getty Images;
Michael Marquand/ Lonely Planet Images/
Getty Images.